# •Fun Stuff•
# Cookies

Publications International, Ltd.

Recipe development on pages 6, 8, 22, 28, 36, 44, 46, 48, 50, 56, 58, 62, 64, 66, 72, 76, 90, 96, 106 and 122 by Jamie Schleser.

Photography on pages 7, 9, 23, 29, 37, 45, 47, 49, 51, 57, 59, 63, 65, 67, 73, 77, 91, 97, 107 and 123 by Laurie Proffitt Photography, Chicago.
**Photographer:** Laurie Proffitt
**Photographer's Assistant:** Chad Evans
**Food Stylist:** Carol Smoler
**Assistant Food Stylist:** Elaine Funk

**Pictured on the front cover:** Easter Nest Cookies *(page 88)*.
**Pictured on the jacket flaps:** Citrus Easter Chicks *(page 16)* and Monogram Cookies *(page 96)*.
**Pictured on the back cover** *(left to right):* Cupcake Cookies *(page 72)*, Kitty Cookies *(page 18)* and Marshmallow Ice Cream Cone Cookies *(page 68)*.

ISBN-13: 978-1-60553-066-6
ISBN-10: 1-60553-066-2

Manufactured in China.

8 7 6 5 4 3 2 1

**Microwave Cooking:** Microwave ovens vary in wattage. Use the cooking times as guidelines and check for doneness before adding more time.

**Preparation/Cooking Times:** Preparation times are based on the approximate amount of time required to assemble the recipe before baking, chilling or serving. These times include preparation steps such as measuring, chopping and mixing. The fact that some preparations and cooking can be done simultaneously is taken into account. Preparation of optional ingredients and serving suggestions is not included.

Publications International, Ltd.

# Contents

# Adorable Animals

## Cookie Dough Bears

1 package (about 16 ounces) refrigerated sugar cookie dough
1 cup uncooked quick oats
   Mini semisweet chocolate chips

**1.** Let dough stand at room temperature 15 minutes. Combine dough and oats in medium bowl; beat with electric mixer at medium speed until blended. Cover and freeze 15 minutes.

**2.** Preheat oven to 350°F. Lightly coat cookie sheets with nonstick cooking spray. For each bear, shape 1 (1-inch) ball for body and 1 (¾-inch) ball for head. Place body and head together on cookie sheets; flatten slightly. Form 7 small balls for arms, legs, ears and nose; arrange on bear body and head. Place 2 chocolate chips on each head for eyes. Place 1 chocolate chip on each body for belly button.

**3.** Bake 12 to 14 minutes or until edges are lightly browned. Cool on cookie sheets 2 minutes. Remove to wire racks; cool completely.                    *Makes about 9 cookies*

**Tip** To make these delicious bears even more fun, try embellishing them with assorted decorating gels. Add a bow tie or a hair bow. Get creative!

# Mischievous Monkeys

   3 cups all-purpose flour
   ½ cup unsweetened cocoa powder
   1 teaspoon salt
   1½ cups sugar
   1 cup (2 sticks) unsalted butter, softened
   2 eggs
   1 teaspoon vanilla
      Yellow gel food coloring
   1 cup prepared white or vanilla frosting
      Black string licorice
   20 brown candy-coated peanut butter candies

1. Whisk flour, cocoa and salt in medium bowl. Beat sugar and butter in large bowl with electric mixer at medium speed until light and fluffy. Add eggs, 1 at a time, beating until blended after each addition. Add vanilla; beat until blended. Gradually add flour mixture, beating until blended after each addition. Divide dough evenly into 2 discs. Wrap and refrigerate 1 hour.

2. Preheat oven to 350°F. Line cookie sheets with parchment paper. Working with 1 disc at a time, roll out dough between parchment paper to ⅜-inch thickness. From each disc, cut out 5 large circles with 3-inch round cookie cutter, 5 medium circles with 2-inch round cookie cutter and 10 small circles with 1½-inch round cookie cutter.

3. Place large circles 3 inches apart on prepared cookie sheets. Place 2 small circles next to each large circle for ears. Place medium circles 1 inch apart on separate prepared cookie sheet. Refrigerate 15 minutes.

4. Bake large circles 15 to 17 minutes or until set. Bake medium circles 12 to 15 minutes or until set. Cool on cookie sheets 5 minutes. Remove to wire racks; cool completely.

5. Add food coloring, a few drops at a time, to frosting; stir until evenly colored. Spread medium circles with frosting. Cut lengths of licorice for nose and mouth; press into frosting. Let stand 10 minutes or until set. Spread thin layer of frosting on back of medium circles and adhere to large circles for mouth. Spread small circle of frosting on inside of each small circle for ears. Dot back of 2 candies with frosting; adhere to each large circle just above medium circle for eyes. Let stand 10 minutes or until set. *Makes 10 cookies*

## •Adorable Animals•

Mischievous Monkeys

# Tasty Turtles

3½ cups all-purpose flour
½ teaspoon salt
1½ cups sugar
1 cup (2 sticks) unsalted butter, softened
2 eggs
2 teaspoons vanilla
Green gel food coloring
144 green gumdrops
Green, black and red decorating gels
Brown candy-coated chocolate pieces
Brown mini candy-coated chocolate pieces

1. Whisk flour and salt in medium bowl. Beat sugar and butter in large bowl with electric mixer at medium speed until light and fluffy. Add eggs, 1 at a time, beating until blended after each addition. Add vanilla; beat until blended.

2. Gradually add flour mixture, beating until blended after each addition. Add food coloring, a few drops at a time, to dough; beat until evenly colored. Divide dough evenly into 2 discs. Wrap and refrigerate 1 hour.

3. Preheat oven to 350°F. Line cookie sheets with parchment paper. Working with 1 disc at a time, cut each disc into 36 even pieces. Roll each piece into a ball; flatten slightly. Place 1 inch apart on prepared cookie sheets. Refrigerate 15 minutes. Bake 12 to 15 minutes or until set. Cool on cookie sheets 5 minutes. Remove to wire racks; cool completely.

4. Reserve 72 gumdrops. Cut remaining gumdrops into quarters. Dot back of gumdrop pieces with green decorating gel and adhere to sides of cookies for legs. Dot bottom of reserved gumdrops with green decorating gel and adhere 1 to each cookie for head. Dot back of 3 chocolate pieces with green decorating gel and adhere to center of each cookie. Dot back of mini chocolate pieces with green decorating gel and adhere to create remainder of shell.

5. Pipe eyes, nose and mouth on each head using black and red decorating gels. Let stand 10 minutes or until set.

*Makes 6 dozen cookies*

Tasty Turtles

# Zebras

2 packages (about 16 ounces each) refrigerated sugar cookie dough
½ cup all-purpose flour
½ cup unsweetened Dutch process cocoa powder
Prepared dark chocolate frosting
Assorted sprinkles
Mini semisweet chocolate chips and semisweet chocolate chips

1. Let doughs stand at room temperature 15 minutes.

2. Combine 1 package dough and flour in large bowl; beat with electric mixer at medium speed until well blended. Combine remaining package dough and cocoa in another large bowl; beat at medium speed until well blended. Form each dough into disc; wrap and freeze 15 minutes.

3. Working with 1 disc at a time, roll out dough between parchment paper into 9-inch square. Place cocoa dough on top of plain dough. Cut into 4 (4½-inch) squares. Layer squares on top of each other, alternating cocoa and plain doughs. Wrap and refrigerate at least 4 hours or up to 2 days.

4. Preheat oven to 350°F. Lightly grease cookie sheets. Trim edges of dough to make square. Cut dough into ¼-inch striped slices, wiping off knife after each cut; cut slices in half to make 2¼×2-inch rectangles. Place rectangles 2 inches apart on prepared cookie sheets.

5. Working with stripes vertically, cut small triangle from top left corner and narrow triangle from top right edge of each rectangle. Discard scraps. Cut small triangle from center of bottom edge; place at top of cookie for ear.

6. Bake 10 minutes or until edges are light brown. Cool on cookie sheets 5 minutes. Remove to wire racks; cool completely.

7. For manes, spread frosting on cookie edges at both sides of ear; top with sprinkles. Attach 1 mini chocolate chip for eye and 1 chocolate chip for nostril to each cookie with frosting.

*Makes about 3 dozen cookies*

Zebras

# Snickerpoodles

1 package (about 16 ounces) refrigerated sugar cookie dough
1 teaspoon ground cinnamon, divided
1 teaspoon vanilla
¼ cup sugar
Semisweet chocolate chips and mini semisweet chocolate chips
White and pink decorating icings

1. Let dough stand at room temperature 15 minutes. Lightly grease cookie sheets.

2. Preheat oven to 350°F. Combine dough, ½ teaspoon cinnamon and vanilla in large bowl; beat with electric mixer at medium speed until well blended. Combine sugar and remaining ½ teaspoon cinnamon in small bowl. For each poodle face, shape 1½ teaspoons dough into oval. Roll in cinnamon-sugar mixture; place on prepared cookie sheets.

3. For poodle ears, divide 1½ teaspoons dough in half; shape each half into teardrop shape. Roll in cinnamon-sugar mixture; place at either side of face.

4. For top of poodle head, shape scant teaspoon dough into oval. Roll in cinnamon-sugar mixture; place at top of face.

5. Bake 10 to 12 minutes or until edges are lightly browned. Immediately press 1 chocolate chip upside down onto each face for nose. Cool on cookie sheets 2 minutes. Remove to wire racks; cool completely.

6. Pipe 2 small circles on each face with white decorating icing. Press mini chocolate chips into icing for eyes. Decorate as desired with white and pink icings.

*Makes about 2 dozen cookies*

Snickerpoodles

# Luscious Lions

## Manes

 1 package (about 16 ounces) refrigerated sugar cookie dough
 ¼ cup all-purpose flour
 2 tablespoons powdered sugar
   Grated peel of 1 large orange
 ¼ teaspoon yellow gel food coloring
 ¼ teaspoon red gel food coloring

## Faces

 1 package (about 16 ounces) refrigerated sugar cookie dough
 ¼ cup all-purpose flour
 2 tablespoons powdered sugar
   Grated peel of 2 lemons
 ½ teaspoon yellow gel food coloring
   Mini candy-coated chocolate pieces
   White decorating icing
   Assorted decors
   Brown decorating icing or melted chocolate

1. For manes, let 1 package dough stand at room temperature 15 minutes. Generously grease 2 cookie sheets.

2. Combine dough, ¼ cup flour, 2 tablespoons powdered sugar, orange peel, ¼ teaspoon yellow food coloring and red food coloring in large bowl; beat with electric mixer at medium speed until well blended. Shape into 24 balls. Place on prepared cookie sheets; flatten into 2¾-inch circles. Cut each circle with 2½-inch fluted round cookie cutter. Discard scraps. Refrigerate 30 minutes.

3. Preheat oven to 350°F. Bake 12 to 14 minutes or until lightly browned. Cool on cookie sheets 2 minutes. Remove to wire racks; cool completely.

4. For faces, let 1 package dough stand at room temperature 15 minutes. Generously grease 2 cookie sheets.

5. Combine dough, ¼ cup flour, 2 tablespoons powdered sugar, lemon peel and ½ teaspoon yellow food coloring in another large bowl; beat with electric mixer at medium speed until well blended. Shape into 24 balls. Place on prepared cookie sheets; flatten into 1¾-inch circles. Cut each circle with 1½-inch round cookie cutter. Remove dough scraps; shape into ears. Attach 2 ears to each face. Place 1 chocolate piece in center of each ear and 1 chocolate piece on face for nose.

6. Bake 14 minutes or until lightly browned. Cool on cookie sheets 2 minutes. Remove to wire racks; cool completely.

7. Attach faces to manes with white decorating icing. Pipe 2 small circles on each face with white icing. Press decors into icing for eyes. Pipe whiskers using brown icing.

*Makes 2 dozen cookies*

## Peppermint Pigs

  1 package (about 16 ounces) refrigerated sugar cookie dough
½ cup all-purpose flour
¾ teaspoon peppermint extract
   Red food coloring
   White decorating icing and mini candy-coated chocolate pieces

1. Let dough stand at room temperature 15 minutes. Lightly grease cookie sheets.

2. Preheat oven to 350°F. Combine dough, flour, peppermint extract and food coloring in large bowl; beat with electric mixer at medium speed until well blended. Divide dough into 20 equal pieces.

3. Shape each dough piece into 1 (1-inch) ball, 1 (½-inch) ball and 2 (¼-inch) balls. Flatten 1-inch ball into ¼-inch-thick circle; place on prepared cookie sheets. Flatten ½-inch ball into ¼-inch-thick oval; place on top of circle for snout. Shape 2 (¼-inch) balls into triangles; fold point over and place at top of circle for ears. Make indentations in snout for nostrils with toothpick.

4. Bake 9 to 11 minutes or until set. Cool on cookie sheets 2 minutes. Remove to wire racks; cool completely. Pipe 2 small circles on each face with white decorating icing. Press chocolate pieces into icing for eyes.

*Makes 20 cookies*

•Adorable Animals•

# Citrus Easter Chicks

1 package (about 16 ounces) refrigerated sugar cookie dough
⅓ cup all-purpose flour
1½ to 2 teaspoons lemon extract
Lemon Cookie Glaze (recipe follows)
2 cups shredded coconut, tinted yellow*
Mini semisweet chocolate chips, assorted candies and decors

*To tint coconut, combine small amount of food coloring (paste, gel or liquid) with 1 teaspoon water in large bowl. Add coconut and stir until evenly coated. Add more food coloring, if needed.*

1. Let dough stand at room temperature 15 minutes. Combine dough, flour and lemon extract in large bowl; beat with electric mixer at medium speed until well blended. Divide dough evenly into 2 discs. Wrap and refrigerate 1 hour.

2. Preheat oven to 350°F. Working with 1 disc at a time, roll out dough between parchment paper to 1/4-inch thickness. Cut out shapes with 2- to 3-inch chick cookie cutters. Place 2 inches apart on ungreased cookie sheets.

3. Bake 7 to 9 minutes or until set. Cool on cookie sheets 5 minutes. Remove to wire racks; cool completely.

4. Place wire racks over parchment paper. Prepare Lemon Cookie Glaze; spread over tops of cookies. Sprinkle with coconut. Decorate chicks with chocolate chips, candies and decors as desired. Let stand 40 minutes or until set. *Makes about 1½ dozen cookies*

# Lemon Cookie Glaze

4 cups powdered sugar
½ teaspoon grated lemon peel
4 to 6 tablespoons lemon juice
Yellow food coloring

Combine powdered sugar, lemon peel and lemon juice, 1 tablespoon at a time, in medium bowl to make pourable glaze. Add food coloring, a few drops at a time; stir until evenly colored. *Makes about 2 cups*

Citrus Easter Chicks

# Kitty Cookies

1 package (about 16 ounces) refrigerated sugar cookie dough
White Decorating Frosting (recipe follows)
Assorted food colorings
Assorted colored candies and red licorice

1. Preheat oven to 350°F. Reserve half of dough; wrap and refrigerate.

2. Roll out remaining dough between parchment paper to $\frac{1}{8}$-inch thickness. Cut out shapes using $3\frac{1}{2}$-inch kitty face cookie cutter. Place 2 inches apart on ungreased cookie sheets. Repeat with reserved dough and scraps.

3. Bake 8 to 10 minutes or until set. Cool on cookie sheets 2 minutes. Remove to wire racks; cool completely.

4. Prepare White Decorating Frosting. Tint with food colorings as desired. Decorate with frosting and assorted candies as desired. Cut licorice into short pieces and press into frosting for whiskers.

*Makes about 1½ dozen cookies*

# White Decorating Frosting

4 cups powdered sugar
½ cup shortening or unsalted butter
1 tablespoon corn syrup
6 to 8 tablespoons milk

Beat powdered sugar, shortening, corn syrup and milk in medium bowl with electric mixer at high speed 2 minutes or until fluffy.

*Makes about 2 cups*

•Adorable Animals•

Birthday Parties Are Lots of Fun!

Kitty Cookies

# Octo-Cookies

  1 package (about 16 ounces) refrigerated chocolate chip cookie dough
  ¼ cup all-purpose flour
 10 whole almonds
    Powdered Sugar Glaze (recipe follows)
    Assorted food colorings
    White decorating icing and assorted candies

1. Let dough stand at room temperature 15 minutes. Grease 10 mini (1¾-inch) muffin cups. Combine dough and flour in large bowl; beat with electric mixer at medium speed until well blended. Reserve two thirds of dough; wrap and refrigerate.

2. Preheat oven to 350°F. For heads, divide remaining one third of dough into 10 equal pieces. Place almond in center of each piece; shape into balls, covering nuts completely. Place in prepared muffin cups; freeze 10 minutes. Bake 10 minutes or until set. Gently loosen cookies around edges; cool in pan 10 minutes. Remove to wire rack; cool completely.

3. For legs, divide reserved dough into 10 equal pieces. Divide each piece equally into 8 pieces; shape each piece into 1½- to 2-inch-long rope. Shape tips at one end to a point. Arrange groups of 8 legs on ungreased cookie sheets with thicker end of legs touching in center and pointed ends about ¼ inch away from each other at outside of circular shape. Bake 6 to 8 minutes or until set. Cool completely on cookie sheets.

4. Place wire racks over waxed paper. Carefully transfer legs to wire racks. Prepare Powdered Sugar Glaze; tint glaze with food colorings as desired. Attach heads to legs using glaze; let stand 15 minutes or until set. Spread remaining glaze over cookies. Let stand 40 minutes or until set. Decorate with white decorating icing and candies as desired.      *Makes 10 cookies*

# Powdered Sugar Glaze

  2 cups powdered sugar
  6 to 9 tablespoons whipping cream, divided

Whisk powdered sugar and 6 tablespoons cream in medium bowl until smooth. Add remaining cream, 1 tablespoon at a time, to make pourable glaze.      *Makes about 1 cup*

## •Adorable Animals•

Octo-Cookies

# Panda Pals

3½ cups all-purpose flour
1 teaspoon salt
1½ cups sugar
1 cup (2 sticks) unsalted butter, softened
2 eggs
1 teaspoon almond extract
1 teaspoon vanilla
1 cup prepared white or vanilla frosting
Black gel food coloring
Black jelly beans, cut in half

1. Whisk flour and salt in medium bowl. Beat sugar and butter in large bowl with electric mixer at medium speed until light and fluffy. Add eggs, 1 at a time, beating until blended after each addition. Add almond extract and vanilla; beat until blended.

2. Gradually add flour mixture, beating until blended after each addition. Divide dough evenly into 2 discs. Wrap and refrigerate 1 hour.

3. Preheat oven to 350°F. Line cookie sheets with parchment paper. Working with 1 disc at a time, roll out dough between parchment paper to ⅜-inch thickness. From each disc, cut out 6 large circles with 3-inch round cookie cutter, 6 medium circles with 1¾-inch round cookie cutter and 12 small circles with 1¼-inch round cookie cutter.

4. Place large circles 3 inches apart on prepared cookie sheets. Place 2 small circles next to each large circle for ears. Place medium circles 1 inch apart on separate prepared cookie sheet. Refrigerate 15 minutes.

5. Bake large circles 15 to 17 minutes or until set. Bake medium circles 12 to 15 minutes or until set. Cool on cookie sheets 5 minutes. Remove to wire racks; cool completely.

6. Spread medium circles with frosting; spread thin layer of frosting on backs and adhere to large circles for mouth. Add food coloring, a few drops at a time, to remaining frosting; stir until evenly colored. Spread small circles with black frosting for ears. Dot cut side of jelly beans with frosting and adhere for eyes and nose. Pipe mouth using black frosting. Let stand 10 minutes or until set.

*Makes 1 dozen cookies*

•Adorable Animals•

Panda Pals

# Just For Kids

## Building Blocks

1 package (about 16 ounces) refrigerated cookie dough, any flavor
Powdered Sugar Glaze (recipe follows)
Assorted food colorings
Assorted small round gummy candies (about ¼ inch in diameter)

**1.** Let dough stand at room temperature 15 minutes. Grease 13×9-inch baking pan.

**2.** Preheat oven to 350°F. Press dough evenly into bottom of prepared pan. Score dough lengthwise and crosswise into 32 equal rectangles (about 2¼×1½ inches each). Freeze 10 minutes.

**3.** Bake 10 minutes. Re-score partially baked cookies. Bake 4 to 5 minutes or until edges are lightly browned and center is set. Cut through score marks to separate cookies. Cool in pan 10 minutes. Remove to wire rack; cool completely.

**4.** Prepare Powdered Sugar Glaze; tint glaze with food colorings as desired. Place wire racks over waxed paper. Spread glaze over tops and sides of cookies. Let stand 5 minutes. Attach 6 gummy candies to each cookie. Let stand 40 minutes or until set.          *Makes 32 cookies*

## Powdered Sugar Glaze

2 cups powdered sugar
6 to 9 tablespoons whipping cream, divided

Whisk powdered sugar and 6 tablespoons cream in medium bowl until smooth. Add remaining cream, 1 tablespoon at a time, to make pourable glaze.          *Makes about 1 cup*

# Cookie Caterpillars

Easy All-Purpose Cookie Dough (recipe follows)
1 cup chocolate hazelnut spread
White chocolate chips, decors, red licorice strings and candy-coated chocolate pieces

**1.** Prepare Easy All-Purpose Cookie Dough.

**2.** Preheat oven to 300°F. Roll out dough between parchment paper to $\frac{1}{4}$-inch thickness. Cut out circles with $1\frac{1}{4}$-inch round cookie cutter. Place 1 inch apart on ungreased cookie sheets.

**3.** Bake 12 to 15 minutes or until tops of cookies are dry to the touch. Cool on cookie sheets 1 minute. Remove to wire racks; cool completely.

**4.** Assemble caterpillars by attaching 7 or 8 cookies together, using chocolate hazelnut spread as "glue" between cookies. Create faces, antennae and legs on caterpillars with chocolate chips, decors, licorice strings and chocolate pieces.    *Makes 12 caterpillars*

# Easy All-Purpose Cookie Dough

1 cup (2 sticks) butter, softened
$\frac{1}{2}$ cup powdered sugar
2 tablespoons packed light brown sugar
$\frac{1}{4}$ teaspoon salt
$\frac{1}{4}$ cup unsweetened Dutch process cocoa powder
1 egg
2 cups all-purpose flour

**1.** Beat butter, powdered sugar, brown sugar and salt in large bowl with electric mixer at medium speed 2 minutes or until light and fluffy. Add cocoa and egg; beat until well blended.

**2.** Add flour, $\frac{1}{2}$ cup at a time, beating well after each addition. Shape dough into disc; wrap and refrigerate 1 hour.

Cookie Caterpillars

# Swashbuckling Pirates

3½ cups all-purpose flour

1 teaspoon salt

1½ cups sugar

1 cup (2 sticks) unsalted butter, softened

2 eggs

2 teaspoons vanilla

Royal Icing (page 30)

Pink, orange, yellow and red gel food colorings

Red string licorice, red candy-coated chocolate pieces and mini semisweet chocolate chips

Black decorating gel

**1.** Whisk flour and salt in medium bowl. Beat sugar and butter in large bowl with electric mixer at medium speed until light and fluffy. Add eggs, 1 at a time, beating until blended after each addition. Add vanilla; beat until blended. Gradually add flour mixture, beating until blended after each addition. Divide dough evenly into 2 discs. Wrap and refrigerate 1 hour.

**2.** Preheat oven to 350°F. Line cookie sheets with parchment paper. Working with 1 disc at a time, roll out dough between parchment paper to ⅜-inch thickness. Cut out circles with 3¼-inch round cookie cutter. Place 1 inch apart on prepared cookie sheets. Refrigerate 15 minutes.

**3.** Bake 15 to 17 minutes or until set. Cool on cookie sheets 5 minutes. Remove to wire racks; cool completely.

**4.** Prepare Royal Icing. Reserve one third of icing in small bowl. Add pink, orange and yellow food colorings, a few drops at a time, to remaining icing to create peach color; stir until evenly colored. Spread two thirds of each cookie with peach icing. Let stand 10 minutes or until set.

**5.** Spread remaining one third of each cookie with reserved white icing. Cut licorice for edge of bandana and mouth; press into icing. Press chocolate pieces into white icing. Let stand 10 minutes or until set.

*continued on page 30*

Swashbuckling Pirates

**6.** Pipe eye patch using decorating gel. Pipe eye with white icing; press mini chocolate chip into center of eye. Press mini chocolate chips into icing for mustache. Let stand 10 minutes or until set.                                                           *Makes about 1½ dozen cookies*

**Royal Icing:** Combine 4 cups powdered sugar, 6 tablespoons water and 3 tablespoons meringue powder in medium bowl. Beat with electric mixer at high speed 7 to 10 minutes or until soft peaks form. Cover surface with plastic wrap until needed. Makes about 2 cups.

# Mud Cups

        1 package (about 16 ounces) refrigerated sugar cookie dough
    ¼ cup unsweetened cocoa powder
        3 containers (4 ounces each) prepared chocolate pudding
    1¼ cups chocolate sandwich cookie crumbs (about 15 cookies)
        Gummy worms

**1.** Let dough stand at room temperature 15 minutes. Grease 18 standard (2½-inch) muffin cups.

**2.** Preheat oven to 350°F. Combine dough and cocoa in large bowl; beat with electric mixer at medium speed until well blended. Shape dough into 18 balls; press onto bottoms and up sides of prepared muffin cups.

**3.** Bake 12 to 14 minutes or until set. Gently press down center of each cookie with back of spoon. Cool in pans 10 minutes. Remove to wire racks; cool completely.

**4.** Fill each cup evenly with pudding; sprinkle with cookie crumbs. Garnish with gummy worms.                                                          *Makes 1½ dozen cookie cups*

**Tip:** Chocolate cookie crumbs can be purchased in the baking section of your supermarket.

Mud Cups

# Peanut Butter Aliens

     1 package (about 16 ounces) refrigerated sugar cookie dough
½ cup creamy peanut butter
⅓ cup all-purpose flour
¼ cup powdered sugar
½ teaspoon vanilla
     Green decorating icing
     1 cup strawberry jam

**1.** Let dough stand at room temperature 15 minutes. Grease 2 cookie sheets.

**2.** Preheat oven to 350°F. Combine dough, peanut butter, flour, powdered sugar and vanilla in large bowl; beat with electric mixer at medium speed until well blended. Reserve half of dough; wrap and refrigerate.

**3.** Roll out remaining dough between parchment paper to ¼-inch thickness. Cut out 14 circles with 3-inch round cookie cutter; pinch 1 side of each circle to make teardrop shape. Place 2 inches apart on prepared cookie sheets. Bake 12 to 14 minutes or until set. Cool on cookie sheets 2 minutes. Remove to wire racks; cool completely.

**4.** Roll out reserved dough between parchment paper to ¼-inch thickness. Cut out 14 circles with 3-inch round cookie cutter; pinch 1 side of each circle to form teardrop shape. Place 2 inches apart on prepared cookie sheets. Cut out 2 oblong holes for eyes. Make small slit for mouth. Bake 12 to 14 minutes or until set. Cool on cookie sheets 2 minutes. Remove to wire racks; cool completely.

**5.** Spread icing on cookies with faces; let stand 10 minutes or until set. Spread jam on uncut cookies. Top each jam-topped cookie with green face cookie.     *Makes 14 sandwich cookies*

Peanut Butter Aliens

# Dinosaur Egg Cookies

      1 cup (2 sticks) margarine or butter, softened
      1 cup confectioners' sugar
      1 egg
      1 teaspoon vanilla
   1½ cups all-purpose flour
   1¼ cups QUAKER® Oats (quick or old fashioned, uncooked)
    ½ cup cornstarch
    ¼ teaspoon salt (optional)
     24 assorted bite-size candies
         Colored sugar or candy sprinkles

**1.** Heat oven to 325°F. Beat margarine and sugar in large bowl with electric mixer until creamy. Add egg and vanilla; beat well. Combine flour, oats, cornstarch and salt, if desired, in medium bowl; mix well. Add to creamed mixture; mix well.

**2.** Shape rounded tablespoonfuls of dough into 1½-inch balls. Press candy piece into center of each ball; shape dough around candy so it is completely hidden. Lightly pinch one side of dough to form egg shape. Roll cookies in desired decorations until evenly coated. Place 2 inches apart on ungreased cookie sheets.

**3.** Bake 16 to 20 minutes or until cookies are set and lightly browned on bottom. Remove to wire rack; cool completely. Store tightly covered.                    *Makes 24 cookies*

Dinosaur Egg Cookies

# Magic Number Cookies

3½ cups all-purpose flour
1 teaspoon salt
1½ cups sugar
1 cup (2 sticks) unsalted butter, softened
2 eggs
2 teaspoons vanilla
Fuschia and teal gel food colorings

**1.** Whisk flour and salt in medium bowl.

**2.** Beat sugar and butter in large bowl with electric mixer at medium speed until light and fluffy. Add eggs, 1 at a time, beating until blended after each addition. Add vanilla; beat until blended.

**3.** Gradually add flour mixture, beating until blended after each addition. Divide dough in half; place in separate medium bowls. Add fuschia food coloring, a few drops at a time, to half of dough; beat until evenly colored. Add teal food coloring, a few drops at a time, to remaining half of dough; beat until evenly colored. Shape each dough into disc; wrap and refrigerate 1 hour.

**4.** Preheat oven to 350°F. Line cookie sheets with parchment paper. Working with 1 disc at a time, roll out dough between parchment paper to ⅜-inch thickness. Cut out stars with 4½-inch cookie cutter. Place 1 inch apart on prepared cookie sheets. Cut out number from center of each star using 2-inch cookie cutter. Transfer fuschia numbers to teal stars and teal numbers to fuschia stars. Refrigerate 15 minutes.

**5.** Bake 15 to 17 minutes or until set. Cool on cookie sheets 5 minutes. Remove to wire racks; cool completely.

*Makes about 14 cookies*

Magic Number Cookies

# Magic Lightning Bolts

1 package (about 16 ounces) refrigerated sugar cookie dough
   Blue food coloring
1 cup prepared cream cheese frosting
   Blue crackling candy or blue decorating sugar

**1.** Grease cookie sheets. Reserve half of dough; wrap and refrigerate.

**2.** Roll out remaining half of dough between parchment paper to ¼-inch thickness. Cut into zigzag lightning shapes about ½ inch wide and 5½ inches long. Place 2 inches apart on prepared cookie sheets. Repeat with reserved dough and scraps. Refrigerate 1 hour.

**3.** Preheat oven to 350°F. Bake 5 to 7 minutes or until edges are lightly browned. Cool on cookie sheets 2 minutes. Remove to wire racks; cool completely.

**4.** Just before serving, add food coloring, a few drops at a time, to frosting; stir until well blended. Spread frosting on cookies. Sprinkle crackling candy over frosting.

*Makes about 2 dozen cookies*

 **Tip** If using crackling candy, do not frost and decorate cookies in advance. Crackling candy begins to lose its popping quality when it is exposed to air and moisture.

Magic Lightning Bolts

# Chocolate Railroad Cookies

2 cups all-purpose flour
¾ cup sugar
½ cup unsweetened cocoa powder
⅛ teaspoon salt
1 cup (2 sticks) unsalted butter, slightly softened, cut into ½-inch pieces

**1.** Beat flour, sugar, cocoa and salt in large bowl with electric mixer at low speed until well combined. With mixer running, add butter, 1 piece at a time, beating until mixture looks moist and crumbly.

**2.** Knead dough with hands until butter is well incorporated. Divide dough in half. Shape each half into rough square; wrap and refrigerate 30 minutes.

**3.** Line 2 cookie sheets with parchment paper. Working with 1 square at a time, roll out dough between parchment paper into 10×6-inch rectangle (about ¼ inch thick). Trim edges, reserving scraps.

**4.** To make rails, cut 2 (¼-inch-wide) strips from the 10-inch side of the rectangle. Place parallel to each other, ½ inch apart, on prepared cookie sheet.

**5.** To make ties, cut off 2 more ¼-inch-wide strips of dough. Cut each strip into 6 pieces (each about 1½ inches long). Press 9 evenly spaced ties across rails. Reserve remaining 3 ties.

**6.** Repeat with remaining dough and reserved scraps to create 6 more railroad tracks. Refrigerate 15 minutes.

**7.** Preheat oven to 350°F. Cut each whole track into 3 separate tracks (3 ties per track), creating 42 cookies total. Arrange cookies ½ inch apart on prepared cookie sheets.

**8.** Bake 12 to 15 minutes or until set. Cool completely on cookie sheets.      *Makes 42 cookies*

Chocolate Railroad Cookies

# Sour Spirals

1 package (about 16 ounces) refrigerated sugar cookie dough
2 tablespoons plus 1½ teaspoons blue raspberry-flavored gelatin
¼ teaspoon blue gel food coloring
2 tablespoons plus 1½ teaspoons strawberry-flavored gelatin
¼ teaspoon pink gel food coloring

**1.** Divide dough in half; place in separate medium bowls. Let stand at room temperature 15 minutes.

**2.** Add blue raspberry gelatin and blue food coloring to dough in one bowl. Add strawberry gelatin and pink food coloring to dough in remaining bowl. Beat doughs separately with electric mixer at medium speed until well blended. Form each dough into disc; wrap and refrigerate 1 hour.

**3.** Roll out blue dough between parchment paper into 10×6-inch rectangle. Repeat with pink dough. Refrigerate both dough rectangles 10 minutes.

**4.** Place blue dough on top of pink dough. Starting at 10-inch side, roll up into tight log. Wrap and freeze 30 minutes.

**5.** Preheat oven to 350°F. Grease cookie sheets. Cut log into ¼-inch slices. Place 1 inch apart on prepared cookie sheets. Bake 8 to 10 minutes or until set. Cool on cookie sheets 2 minutes. Remove to wire racks; cool completely.          *Makes 40 cookies*

# Cheery Chocolate Animal Cookies

1⅔ cups (10-ounce package) REESE'S® Peanut Butter Chips
1 cup HERSHEY'S SPECIAL DARK® Chocolate Chips or HERSHEY'S Semi-Sweet Chocolate Chips
2 tablespoons shortening (do not use butter, margarine, spread or oil)
1 package (20 ounces) chocolate sandwich cookies
1 package (11 ounces) animal crackers

*continued on page 44*

Sour Spirals

*Cheery Chocolate Animal Cookies, continued*

**1.** Line trays or cookie sheets with wax paper.

**2.** Combine peanut butter chips, chocolate chips and shortening in 2-quart glass measuring cup with handle. Microwave at MEDIUM (50%) 1½ to 2 minutes or until chips are melted and mixture is smooth when stirred. Using fork, dip each cookie into melted chip mixture; gently tap fork on side of cup to remove excess chocolate.

**3.** Place coated cookies on prepared trays; top each cookie with an animal cracker. Chill until chocolate is set, about 30 minutes. Store in airtight container in a cool, dry place.

*Makes about 4 dozen cookies*

# Treasure Chests

   1 package (about 19 ounces) brownie mix, plus ingredients to prepare mix
   1 container (16 ounces) chocolate frosting
 24 fudge-covered graham crackers
    Yellow decorating icing
    Mini candy-coated chocolate pieces
    Yellow decorating gel

**1.** Preheat oven to 350°F. Coat 9-inch square baking pan with nonstick cooking spray.

**2.** Prepare brownie mix according to package directions; pour batter into prepared pan. Bake 35 minutes or until toothpick inserted into center comes out clean. Cool completely in pan on wire rack. Cover; freeze 1 hour or overnight.

**3.** Run knife around edges of brownies. Place cutting board over baking pan; invert and let stand until brownies release from pan. Trim edges; discard. Cut into 24 rectangles.

**4.** Spread tops and sides of brownies with frosting. Let stand on wire racks 10 minutes or until set. Pipe lines on brownies and graham crackers with decorating icing to resemble chests.

**5.** Dot back of chocolate pieces with decorating gel; adhere on front half of brownie tops for treasure. Spread 1 edge of each graham cracker with frosting; adhere 1 graham cracker to back half of each brownie top so that it leans on chocolate pieces. Let stand 10 minutes or until set.

*Makes 2 dozen brownies*

Treasure Chests

# Fun & Games

## Silly Sunglasses

3½ cups all-purpose flour
½ teaspoon salt
1½ cups sugar
1 cup (2 sticks) unsalted butter, softened
2 eggs
2 teaspoons vanilla
24 to 32 fruit-flavored hard candies, crushed
Assorted colored decorating icings
Assorted decors

**1.** Whisk flour and salt in medium bowl.

**2.** Beat sugar and butter in large bowl with electric mixer at medium speed until light and fluffy. Add eggs, 1 at a time, beating until blended after each addition. Add vanilla; beat until blended.

**3.** Gradually add flour mixture, beating until blended after each addition. Divide dough evenly into 2 discs. Wrap and refrigerate 1 hour.

**4.** Preheat oven to 350°F. Line cookie sheets with silicone mats or parchment paper. Working with 1 disc at a time, roll out dough between parchment paper to ¼-inch thickness. Cut out sunglasses shapes with sharp knife (approximately 4×2-inch shapes). Place 2 inches apart on prepared cookie sheets. Cut out lenses from sunglasses; discard. Refrigerate 15 minutes.

**5.** Sprinkle crushed candy into each opening. Bake 10 minutes or until candy is melted and cookies are set. Cool completely on cookie sheets. Decorate sunglasses with decorating icings and decors as desired.

*Makes 12 to 16 cookies*

# Billiard Balls

3½ cups all-purpose flour
1 teaspoon salt
1½ cups sugar
1 cup (2 sticks) unsalted butter, softened
2 eggs
2 teaspoons vanilla
2 containers (16 ounces each) white or vanilla frosting
Assorted gel food colorings
Black decorating icing

**1.** Whisk flour and salt in medium bowl. Beat sugar and butter in large bowl with electric mixer at medium speed until light and fluffy. Add eggs, 1 at a time, beating until blended after each addition. Add vanilla; beat until blended.

**2.** Gradually add flour mixture, beating until blended after each addition. Divide dough evenly into 2 discs. Wrap and refrigerate 1 hour.

**3.** Preheat oven to 350°F. Line cookie sheets with parchment paper. Working with 1 disc at a time, roll out dough between parchment paper to ⅜-inch thickness. Cut out 18 large circles with 3-inch round cookie cutter. Place 1 inch apart on prepared cookie sheets. Cut out 18 small circles with 1¼-inch round cookie cutter. Place 1 inch apart on separate prepared cookie sheet. Refrigerate 15 minutes.

**4.** Bake large circles 15 to 17 minutes or until set. Bake small circles 12 to 15 minutes or until set. Cool on cookie sheets 5 minutes. Remove to wire racks; cool completely.

**5.** Reserve one fourth of frosting. Divide remaining frosting evenly among small bowls and tint with food colorings to make desired colors. For "solids," spread large circles with tinted frosting. Let stand 10 minutes or until set.

**6.** For "stripes," spread center two thirds of each large circle with tinted frosting. Let stand 10 minutes or until set. Spread remaining one third of each large circle with reserved white frosting. Let stand 10 minutes or until set.

**7.** Spread small circles with remaining white frosting. Pipe number in center of each white circle using decorating icing. Spread thin layer of frosting on back of small circles and adhere to center of large circles. Let stand 10 minutes or until set. *Makes 1½ dozen cookies*

*·Fun & Games·*

Billiard Balls

# Palm Trees

1 package (about 16 ounces) refrigerated break-apart sugar cookie dough (24 count)
1 container (16 ounces) white or vanilla frosting
Green and brown gel food colorings
Green sparkling sugar
Assorted colored candy-coated sunflower seeds (optional)

**1.** Let dough stand at room temperature 5 minutes. Line cookie sheets with parchment paper.

**2.** Preheat oven to 325°F. Roll out dough between parchment paper to ¼-inch thickness. Cut out palm tree shapes with sharp knife (approximately 3×3-inch shapes). Place 2 inches apart on prepared cookie sheets. Refrigerate 15 minutes.

**3.** Bake 13 to 15 minutes or until set. Cool on cookie sheets 5 minutes. Remove to wire racks; cool completely.

**4.** Reserve half of frosting in small bowl. Add green food coloring, a few drops at a time, to remaining frosting; stir until evenly colored. Spread leafy part of cookies with green frosting. Sprinkle with sparkling sugar. Add sunflower seeds, if desired. Let stand 10 minutes or until set.

**5.** Add brown food coloring, a few drops at a time, to reserved frosting. Spread trunks of cookies with brown frosting. Use toothpick to create rough texture. Let stand 10 minutes or until set.

*Makes about 16 cookies*

Palm Trees

# Nothin' but Net

1 package (about 16 ounces) refrigerated sugar cookie dough
1¼ cups all-purpose flour
2 tablespoons powdered sugar
2 tablespoons lemon juice
Orange, white and black decorating icings

**1.** Let dough stand at room temperature 15 minutes.

**2.** Combine dough, flour, powdered sugar and lemon juice in large bowl; beat with electric mixer at medium speed until well blended. Divide dough evenly into 2 discs. Wrap and refrigerate at least 2 hours.

**3.** Preheat oven to 350°F. Lightly grease cookie sheets. Working with 1 disc at a time, roll out dough between parchment paper to ¼-inch thickness. Cut out basketball-in-net shapes. Place 2 inches apart on prepared cookie sheets.

**4.** Bake 13 to 15 minutes or until edges are lightly browned. Remove to wire racks; cool completely. Decorate with icings.
*Makes 1½ dozen cookies*

**Tip** These cookies would be perfect for a sports-themed birthday party. Try serving them with Snickerdoodle Batter Ups (page 55) and Nutty Footballs (page 60).

Nothin' but Net

# Tic-Tac-Toe Cookies

¾ cup (1½ sticks) butter, softened
¾ cup granulated sugar
1 large egg
1 teaspoon vanilla extract
2¼ cups all-purpose flour
½ teaspoon baking powder
¼ teaspoon salt
4 squares (1 ounce each) semi-sweet chocolate, melted
¼ cup powdered sugar
1 teaspoon water
½ cup "M&M's"® Chocolate Mini Baking Bits

In large bowl cream butter and granulated sugar until light and fluffy; beat in egg and vanilla. In small bowl combine flour, baking powder and salt; blend into creamed mixture. Reserve half of dough. Stir chocolate into remaining dough. Wrap and refrigerate doughs 30 minutes. Working with one dough at a time on lightly floured surface, roll or pat into 7×4½-inch rectangle. Cut dough into 9 (7×½-inch) strips. Repeat with remaining dough. Place one strip chocolate dough on sheet of plastic wrap. Place one strip vanilla dough next to chocolate dough. Place second strip of chocolate dough next to vanilla dough to make bottom layer. Prepare second row by stacking strips on first row, alternating vanilla dough over chocolate, and chocolate dough over vanilla. Repeat with third row to complete 1 bar. Repeat entire process with remaining dough strips, starting with vanilla dough, to complete second bar. Wrap both bars and refrigerate 1 hour. Preheat oven to 350°F. Lightly grease cookie sheets. Cut bars crosswise into ¼-inch slices. Place 2 inches apart on prepared cookie sheets. Bake 10 to 12 minutes. Cool on cookie sheets 2 minutes; cool completely on wire racks. In small bowl combine powdered sugar and water until smooth. Using icing to attach, decorate cookies with "M&M's"® Chocolate Mini Baking Bits to look like Tic-Tac-Toe games. Store in tightly covered container.

*Makes 4 dozen cookies*

# Snickerdoodle Batter Ups

1 package (about 16 ounces) refrigerated sugar cookie dough
1 teaspoon vanilla
¼ cup sugar
¼ teaspoon ground cinnamon
Brown and red decorating icings

**1.** Let dough stand at room temperature 15 minutes.

**2.** Combine dough and vanilla in large bowl; beat with electric mixer at medium speed until well blended. Divide dough evenly into 2 discs; wrap and refrigerate 1 hour.

**3.** Preheat oven to 350°F. For baseballs, roll out 1 disc dough between parchment paper to ¼-inch thickness. Cut out circles using 2½-inch round cookie cutter. Re-roll scraps, if necessary, to make a total of 12 circles. Place 2 inches apart on ungreased cookie sheet.

**4.** Combine sugar and cinnamon in small bowl. Sprinkle each cutout with ½ teaspoon cinnamon-sugar. Bake 8 to 10 minutes or until edges are lightly browned. Cool on cookie sheet 3 minutes. Remove to wire rack; cool completely.

**5.** For bats, roll out remaining 1 disc dough between parchment paper to ¼-inch thickness. Cut out 4-inch bat shapes using sharp knife. Re-roll scraps, if necessary, to make a total of 12 bats. Place 2 inches apart on ungreased cookie sheet.

**6.** Sprinkle each cutout with ½ teaspoon cinnamon-sugar. Bake 8 to 10 minutes or until edges are lightly browned. Cool on cookie sheet 3 minutes. Remove to wire rack; cool completely.

**7.** Pipe brown icing onto bat cookies to resemble tape on handles. Pipe red icing onto balls to resemble seams.

*Makes 2 dozen cookies*

# Go Fly a Kite Cookies

3½ cups all-purpose flour
1 teaspoon salt
1½ cups sugar
1 cup (2 sticks) unsalted butter, softened
2 eggs
2 teaspoons vanilla
Royal Icing (recipe follows)
Blue and green gel food colorings
Yellow decorating icing

**1.** Whisk flour and salt in medium bowl. Beat sugar and butter in large bowl with electric mixer at medium speed until light and fluffy. Add eggs, 1 at a time, beating until blended after each addition. Add vanilla; beat until blended. Gradually add flour mixture, beating until blended after each addition. Divide dough evenly into 2 discs. Wrap and refrigerate 1 hour.

**2.** Preheat oven to 350°F. Line cookie sheets with parchment paper. Working with 1 disc at a time, roll out dough between parchment paper to ⅜-inch thickness. Cut out circles with 3¼-inch round cookie cutter. Place 1 inch apart on prepared cookie sheets. Refrigerate 15 minutes.

**3.** Bake 15 to 17 minutes or until set. Cool on cookie sheets 5 minutes. Remove to wire racks; cool completely.

**4.** Prepare Royal Icing. Reserve ¾ cup Royal Icing. Add blue food coloring, a few drops at a time, to remaining icing to create sky blue; stir until evenly colored. Spread cookies with sky blue icing. Let stand 10 minutes or until set.

**5.** Pipe clouds using ¼ cup reserved white icing. Divide remaining ½ cup white icing into 2 small bowls. Add food coloring, a drop at a time, to each bowl to make dark blue and green icings. Pipe kites using dark blue and green icings. Pipe kite tails using yellow decorating icing. Let stand 10 minutes or until set. *Makes about 1½ dozen cookies*

Royal Icing: Combine 4 cups powdered sugar, 6 tablespoons water and 3 tablespoons meringue powder in medium bowl. Beat with electric mixer at high speed 7 to 10 minutes or until soft peaks form. Cover surface with plastic wrap until needed. Makes about 2 cups.

·Fun & Games·

Go Fly a Kite Cookies

# Poker Night Cookies

3½ cups all-purpose flour
½ teaspoon salt
1½ cups sugar
1 cup (2 sticks) unsalted butter, softened
2 eggs
2 teaspoons vanilla
Red and black gel food colorings

**1.** Whisk flour and salt in medium bowl.

**2.** Beat sugar and butter in large bowl with electric mixer at medium speed until light and fluffy. Add eggs, 1 at a time, beating until blended after each addition. Add vanilla; beat until blended.

**3.** Gradually add flour mixture, beating until blended after each addition. Divide dough in half; place in 2 separate medium bowls. Add red food coloring, a few drops at a time, to half of dough; beat until evenly colored. Add black food coloring, a few drops at a time, to remaining half of dough; beat until evenly colored. Shape each dough into disc; wrap and refrigerate 1 hour.

**4.** Preheat oven to 350°F. Line cookie sheets with parchment paper. Working with 1 disc at a time, roll out dough between parchment paper to ⅜-inch thickness. Cut out circles with 3-inch round cookie cutter. Place 1 inch apart on prepared cookie sheets. Cut out hearts, clubs, diamonds or spades from centers of circles using 1-inch card suite cookie cutters. Transfer red shapes to black circles and black shapes to red circles. Refrigerate 15 minutes.

**5.** Bake 15 to 17 minutes or until set. Cool on cookie sheets 5 minutes. Remove to wire racks; cool completely.

*Makes 2 dozen cookies*

Poker Night Cookies

# Nutty Footballs

2 cups all-purpose flour
¼ cup unsweetened cocoa powder
1 cup (2 sticks) butter, softened
½ cup sugar
1 egg
½ teaspoon vanilla
1 cup finely chopped almonds
Assorted colored decorating icings (optional)
White decorating icing

**1.** Combine flour and cocoa in small bowl. Beat butter and sugar in large bowl with electric mixer at medium speed until light and fluffy. Add egg and vanilla; beat until well blended. Gradually add flour mixture, beating until blended after each addition. Add almonds; beat until well blended. Shape dough into disc. Wrap and refrigerate 30 minutes.

**2.** Preheat oven to 350°F. Lightly grease cookie sheets. Roll out dough between parchment paper to ¼-inch thickness. Cut out shapes with 2½- to 3-inch football cookie cutter.* Place 2 inches apart on prepared cookie sheets. Refrigerate 15 minutes.

**3.** Bake 10 to 12 minutes or until set. Cool on cookie sheets 2 minutes. Remove to wire racks; cool completely. Decorate with colored icings, if desired. Pipe white icing onto footballs to resemble laces.                                      *Makes 2 dozen cookies*

*To make football shapes without a cookie cutter, shape 3 tablespoonfuls of dough into ovals. Place 3 inches apart on prepared cookie sheets. Flatten ovals to ¼-inch thickness; taper ends.*

Nutty Footballs

# Flip-Flops

1 package (about 16 ounces) refrigerated break-apart sugar cookie dough (24 count)
1 container (16 ounces) white or vanilla frosting
  Assorted gel food colorings
  Red string licorice
  Edible cake decorations*
  Star-shaped candy sprinkles

*Edible cake decorations are made from molded sugar. They can be found in the baking aisle at large supermarkets, party supply stores and craft stores.*

**1.** Let dough stand at room temperature 5 minutes. Line cookie sheets with parchment paper.

**2.** Preheat oven to 325°F. Roll out dough between parchment paper to ¼-inch thickness. Cut out flip-flop shapes with sharp knife (approximately 3×1½-inch shapes). Place 2 inches apart on prepared cookie sheets. Refrigerate 15 minutes.

**3.** Bake 13 to 15 minutes or until set. Cool on cookie sheets 5 minutes. Remove to wire racks; cool completely.

**4.** Divide frosting evenly among small bowls and tint with food colorings to make desired colors. Spread cookies with frosting. Cut licorice for straps; press into frosting. Top with cake decorations. Decorate with candy sprinkles as desired. Let stand 10 minutes or until set.

*Makes about 20 cookies*

 **Tip** Flip-flops come in hundreds of colors and designs, so feel free to experiment with frosting colors, fun stripes or swirls in the frosting or even other kinds of sprinkles and candies to make pretty patterns.

Flip-Flops

# Favorite Foods

1 package (about 19 ounces) brownie mix, plus ingredients to prepare mix
1 package (14 ounces) milk chocolate or peanut butter candy discs
½ (16-ounce) container white or vanilla frosting
   Colored drinking straws
   Colored sprinkles

1. Preheat oven to 350°F. Coat 9-inch square baking pan with nonstick cooking spray.

2. Prepare brownie mix according to package directions; pour batter into prepared pan. Bake 35 minutes or until toothpick inserted into center comes out clean. Cool completely in pan on wire rack. Cover; freeze 1 hour or overnight.

3. Run knife around edges of brownies. Place cutting board over baking pan; invert and let stand until brownies release from pan. Trim edges; discard. Cut into 18 rectangles.

4. Microwave candy discs in medium microwavable bowl on HIGH 1 minute. Stir. Microwave at additional 15-second intervals until smooth and spreadable. Stand brownies up on small side. Spread all sides except bottom of brownies with candy mixture. Let stand on wire racks 10 minutes or until set.

5. Pipe frosting on top of each brownie for whipped cream. Decorate with straws and sprinkles.

*Makes 1½ dozen brownies*

# Over Easy Cookies

1 package (about 16 ounces) refrigerated break-apart sugar cookie dough (24 count)
1 package (14 ounces) white chocolate candy discs
   Yellow gel food coloring
1 cup prepared white or vanilla frosting

1. Let dough stand at room temperature 5 minutes. Line cookie sheets with parchment paper.

2. Preheat oven to 325°F. Roll out dough between parchment paper to ¼-inch thickness. Cut out egg white shapes with sharp knife (approximately 2½×3½-inch shapes). Place egg whites 2 inches apart on prepared cookie sheets. Cut out yolks with 1¼-inch round cookie cutter. Place egg yolks 1 inch apart on separate prepared cookie sheet. Refrigerate 15 minutes.

3. Bake egg whites 15 to 17 minutes or until set. Bake egg yolks 10 to 12 minutes or until set. Cool on cookie sheets 5 minutes. Remove to wire racks; cool completely.

4. Microwave candy discs in medium microwavable bowl on HIGH 1 minute. Stir. Microwave at additional 15-second intervals until smooth and spreadable. Spread egg whites with candy mixture. Let stand on wire racks 10 minutes or until set.

5. Add food coloring, a few drops at a time, to frosting; stir until evenly colored. Spread egg yolks with yellow frosting. Spread thin layer of frosting on back of egg yolks and adhere to egg whites. Let stand 10 minutes or until set.           *Makes about 1 dozen cookies*

# Tiny Hot Fudge Sundae Cups

1 package (about 16 ounces) refrigerated sugar cookie dough
⅓ cup unsweetened cocoa powder
5 to 7 cups vanilla ice cream
   Hot fudge ice cream topping, colored sprinkles and aerosol whipped cream
9 maraschino cherries, cut into quarters

1. Let dough stand at room temperature 15 minutes. Spray outsides of 36 mini (1¾-inch) muffin cups with nonstick cooking spray.

*continued on page 68*

•favorite foods•

Over Easy Cookies, Makin' Bacon Cookies (page 76)

*Tiny Hot Fudge Sundae Cups, continued*

2. Preheat oven to 350°F. Combine dough and cocoa in large bowl; beat with electric mixer at medium speed until well blended. Divide dough into 36 equal pieces; shape each piece over outside of prepared muffin cup. Bake 10 to 12 minutes or until set. Cool on pans 10 minutes. Remove to wire racks; cool completely.

3. Fill cookie cups evenly with ice cream. Drizzle with hot fudge sauce; top with sprinkles. Garnish each sundae cup with whipped cream and cherry quarter. Serve immediately.

*Makes 3 dozen sundae cups*

# Marshmallow Ice Cream Cone Cookies

    1 package (about 16 ounces) refrigerated sugar cookie dough
    6 ice cream sugar cones, broken into pieces
    1 container (16 ounces) white frosting
    1 package (about 10 ounces) colored miniature marshmallows
    Colored sprinkles

1. Let dough stand at room temperature 15 minutes.

2. Preheat oven to 350°F. Place sugar cones in food processor. Process using on/off pulsing action until finely ground. Combine dough and sugar cones in large bowl; beat until well blended.

3. Shape dough into 3 equal balls. Pat each ball into 9-inch circle on lightly floured surface. Cut each circle into 6 wedges; place 2 inches apart on ungreased cookie sheets.

4. Bake 10 to 11 minutes or until edges are lightly browned. While cookies are still warm, score crisscross pattern into cookies. Cool on cookie sheets 5 minutes. Remove cookies to wire racks; cool completely.

5. Spread 2-inch strip of frosting at wide end of each cookie. Press marshmallows into frosting; top with sprinkles.

*Makes 1½ dozen cookies*

Marshmallow Ice Cream Cone Cookies

# Peanut Butter & Jelly Sandwich Cookies

1 package (about 16 ounces) refrigerated sugar cookie dough
1 tablespoon unsweetened cocoa powder
¾ cup creamy peanut butter
½ cup grape jelly

1. Reserve three fourths of dough; wrap and refrigerate. Beat remaining one fourth of dough and cocoa in small bowl with electric mixer at medium speed until well blended; cover and refrigerate.

2. Shape reserved dough into 5½-inch log. Roll out chocolate dough between parchment paper into 9½×6½-inch rectangle. Place log in center of rectangle.

3. Bring chocolate dough up and over log so log is wrapped in chocolate dough; press edges to seal. Flatten top and sides of dough slightly to form square. Wrap and freeze 10 minutes.

4. Preheat oven to 350°F. Cut dough into ¼-inch slices. Place 2 inches apart on ungreased cookie sheets. Reshape dough edges into square, if necessary. Press edge of dough slightly to form indentation so dough resembles slice of bread.

5. Bake 8 to 11 minutes or until lightly browned. Immediately straighten cookie edges with spatula. Cool on cookie sheets 2 minutes. Remove to wire racks; cool completely.

6. Spread peanut butter on half of cookies. Spread jelly over peanut butter; top with remaining cookies, pressing gently.                    *Makes 11 sandwich cookies*

Peanut Butter & Jelly Sandwich Cookies

# Cupcake Cookies

    3½ cups all-purpose flour
    1 teaspoon salt
    1½ cups sugar
    1 cup (2 sticks) unsalted butter, softened
    2 eggs
    2 teaspoons vanilla
    1½ containers (16 ounces each) white or vanilla frosting
        Assorted gel food colorings
        Large confetti sprinkles

1. Whisk flour and salt in medium bowl.

2. Beat sugar and butter in large bowl with electric mixer at medium speed until light and fluffy. Add eggs, 1 at a time, beating until blended after each addition. Add vanilla; beat until blended.

3. Gradually add flour mixture, beating until blended after each addition. Divide dough evenly into 2 discs. Wrap and refrigerate 1 hour.

4. Preheat oven to 350°F. Line cookie sheets with parchment paper. Working with 1 disc at a time, roll out dough between parchment paper to ⅜-inch thickness. Cut out cupcake shapes with sharp knife (approximately 2½×2½-inch shapes). Place 1 inch apart on prepared cookie sheets. Refrigerate 15 minutes.

5. Bake 15 to 17 minutes or until set. Cool on cookie sheets 5 minutes. Remove to wire racks; cool completely.

6. Reserve half of frosting. Add food coloring, a few drops at a time, to remaining half of frosting; stir until evenly colored. Spread bottom half of cookies with frosting. Let stand 3 minutes or until just beginning to set. Press toothpick into frosting to create lines that resemble paper liner cups. Let stand on wire racks 10 minutes or until set.

7. Add food coloring, a few drops at a time, to reserved frosting; stir until evenly colored. (Divide frosting before adding food coloring if more colors are desired.) Spread top half of cookies with frosting. Press sprinkles into frosting. Let stand 10 minutes or until set.

*Makes 2 dozen cookies*

·Favorite Foods·

# Watermelon Slices

    2 packages (about 16 ounces each) refrigerated sugar cookie dough
    ½ cup all-purpose flour, divided
        Green and red food colorings
        Mini chocolate chips

1. Let doughs stand at room temperature 15 minutes.

2. Combine 1 package dough, ¼ cup flour and green food coloring in large bowl; beat with electric mixer at medium speed until well blended. Wrap and refrigerate 2 hours.

3. Combine remaining package dough, remaining ¼ cup flour and red food coloring in separate large bowl; beat at medium speed until well blended. Shape into 9-inch-long log. Wrap and refrigerate 2 hours.

4. Roll out green dough between parchment paper into 9×8-inch rectangle. Place log in center of green rectangle. Fold edges up and around log; press edges to seal. Roll gently to form smooth log. Wrap and freeze 30 minutes.

5. Preheat oven to 350°F. Cut log into ⅜-inch-thick slices. Cut each slice in half. Place 2 inches apart on ungreased cookie sheets. Gently reshape, if necessary. Press several mini chocolate chips into each slice for watermelon seeds.

6. Bake 8 to 11 minutes or until set. Cool on cookie sheets 1 minute. Remove to wire racks; cool completely.                                              *Makes about 4 dozen cookies*

Watermelon Slices

# Makin' Bacon Cookies

  1 package (about 16 ounces) refrigerated break-apart sugar cookie dough (24 count)
½ cup water, divided
  Red, brown and yellow gel food colorings

1. Let dough stand at room temperature 5 minutes. Line cookie sheets with parchment paper.

2. Preheat oven to 325°F. Roll out dough between parchment paper to ¼-inch thickness. Cut out bacon shapes with sharp knife (approximately 1×3½-inch shapes). Place 2 inches apart on prepared cookie sheets. Refrigerate 15 minutes.

3. Bake 13 to 15 minutes or until set. Cool on cookie sheets 5 minutes. Remove to wire racks; cool completely.

4. Place ¼ cup water in small bowl. Add a few drops of red and brown food colorings; stir until evenly colored. Place remaining ¼ cup water in another small bowl. Add a few drops of red and yellow food colorings; stir until evenly colored. Paint cookies to resemble bacon with small clean paintbrushes,* using as little water as possible for color to saturate. Leave some areas unpainted to resemble bacon fat. Let stand 1 hour or until dry.

*Makes about 2 dozen cookies*

*Do not use paintbrushes that have been used for anything other than food.*

Makin' Bacon Cookies

# Burger Bliss

## Buns

1 package (about 16 ounces) refrigerated sugar cookie dough
½ cup creamy peanut butter
⅓ cup all-purpose flour
¼ cup packed brown sugar
½ teaspoon vanilla
Beaten egg white and sesame seeds (optional)

## Burgers

½ (16-ounce) package refrigerated sugar cookie dough*
3 tablespoons unsweetened cocoa powder
2 tablespoons packed brown sugar
½ teaspoon vanilla
Red, yellow and green decorating icings

*Reserve remaining dough for another use.*

1. Preheat oven to 350°F. Grease cookie sheets.

2. For buns, let 1 package dough stand at room temperature 15 minutes. Combine dough, peanut butter, flour, ¼ cup brown sugar and ½ teaspoon vanilla in large bowl; beat with electric mixer at medium speed until well blended. Shape into 48 (1-inch) balls; place 2 inches apart on prepared cookie sheets.

3. Bake 14 minutes or until lightly browned. Brush half of cookies with egg white and sprinkle with sesame seeds after 10 minutes, if desired. Cool on cookie sheets 2 minutes. Remove to wire racks; cool completely.

4. For burgers, let ½ package dough stand at room temperature 15 minutes. Combine dough, cocoa, 2 tablespoons brown sugar and ½ teaspoon vanilla in medium bowl; beat with electric mixer at medium speed until well blended. Shape into 24 (1-inch) balls; place 2 inches apart on prepared cookie sheets. Flatten to ¼-inch thickness.

5. Bake 12 minutes or until set. Cool on cookie sheets 2 minutes. Remove to wire racks; cool completely. To assemble, use icing to attach burgers to flat sides of 24 buns. Pipe red, yellow and green icings on burgers. Top with remaining buns. *Makes 2 dozen sandwich cookies*

Burger Bliss

# Citrus Slices

1 package (about 16 ounces) refrigerated sugar cookie dough
3 tablespoons all-purpose flour
½ teaspoon lemon extract
  Yellow, green and orange food colorings
1 egg white, lightly beaten
  Yellow, green and orange decorating sugars
½ teaspoon lime extract
½ teaspoon orange extract
  Coarse white decorating sugar

1. Let dough stand at room temperature 15 minutes.

2. Combine dough and flour in large bowl; beat with electric mixer at medium speed until well blended. Divide dough into 3 equal pieces.

3. Add lemon extract and yellow food coloring to 1 dough piece in medium bowl; beat until well blended. Shape dough into 6×1½-inch log; flatten 1 side of log to make half-moon shape. Brush rounded side of log with egg white; sprinkle with yellow sugar until evenly coated. Wrap and freeze 1 hour.

4. Repeat step 3 with second piece of dough, lime extract, green food coloring and green sugar.

5. Repeat step 3 with remaining piece of dough, orange extract, orange food coloring and orange sugar.

6. Preheat oven to 350°F. Lightly grease cookie sheets. Cut logs into ¼-inch slices; place 2 inches apart on prepared cookie sheets. Sprinkle with coarse white sugar.

7. Bake 9 to 11 minutes or until set. Immediately score hot cookies. Cool on cookie sheets 2 minutes. Remove to wire racks; cool completely.           *Makes 6 dozen cookies*

Citrus Slices

# Let's Celebrate

## Window-to-My-Heart Cookies

2¼ cups all-purpose flour
½ teaspoon salt
¼ teaspoon baking powder
1 cup (2 sticks) butter, softened
½ cup powdered sugar
¼ cup packed brown sugar
1 teaspoon vanilla
1 cup sweetened dried cranberries, chopped
15 to 20 cherry- or cinnamon-flavored hard candies, crushed

**1.** Combine flour, salt and baking powder in medium bowl. Beat butter, powdered sugar, brown sugar and vanilla in large bowl with electric mixer at medium speed until creamy. Gradually add flour mixture, beating until blended after each addition. Stir in cranberries. Shape dough into disc; wrap and refrigerate 1 hour.

**2.** Preheat oven to 325°F. Line cookie sheets with silicone mats or parchment paper. Roll out dough between parchment paper to ¼-inch thickness. Cut out shapes using 2- to 3-inch heart cookie cutter. Cut out center of each cookie using smaller heart cookie cutter; re-roll scraps to make additional hearts.

**3.** Place 1 inch apart on prepared cookie sheets. Sprinkle crushed candy into each opening. Bake 20 minutes or until candy is melted and cookies are set. Cool completely on cookie sheets.

*Makes about 3 dozen cookies*

# Masquerade Party Cookies

1 package (about 16 ounces) refrigerated chocolate chip cookie dough
¼ cup all-purpose flour
Colored nonpareils
Black decorating icing
Red string licorice, cut into 5-inch lengths

**1.** Let dough stand at room temperature 15 minutes. Lightly grease cookie sheets.

**2.** Preheat oven to 350°F. Combine dough and flour in large bowl; beat with electric mixer at medium speed until well blended.

**3.** Shape dough into 20 (3-inch long) ovals; roll in nonpareils. Place 2 inches apart on prepared cookie sheets; flatten slightly. Pinch ovals in at centers to create mask shapes. Decorate with additional nonpareils.

**4.** Bake 8 to 10 minutes or until edges are lightly browned. Make oval indentations for eyes with back of spoon. Reshape at centers, if necessary. Cool completely on cookie sheets.

**5.** Spread eye area with icing. Attach licorice piece to each side of mask with icing. Let stand 15 minutes or until set.

*Makes 20 cookies*

 **Tip** If you can't find colored nonpareils, you can use other sprinkles, candies or decorating gels to customize the look and color scheme of these whimsical cookies.

Masquerade Party Cookies

# White Chocolate Shamrocks

    2 packages (about 16 ounces each) refrigerated sugar cookie dough
½ cup all-purpose flour
    Green food coloring
 1 package (14 ounces) white chocolate candy discs
    Green and white sprinkles, dragées or colored sugar

**1.** Let doughs stand at room temperature 15 minutes. Lightly grease cookie sheets.

**2.** Preheat oven to 350°F. Beat doughs, flour and food coloring, a few drops at a time, in large bowl with electric mixer at medium speed until well blended. Reserve half of dough; wrap and refrigerate.

**3.** Roll out remaining dough between parchment paper to ¼-inch thickness. Cut out shapes using 2-inch shamrock cookie cutter. Place 2 inches apart on prepared cookie sheets. Repeat with reserved dough. Refrigerate 15 minutes.

**4.** Bake 8 to 10 minutes or until set. Cool on cookie sheets 5 minutes. Remove to wire racks; cool completely.

**5.** Microwave candy discs in medium microwavable bowl on HIGH 1 minute. Stir. Microwave at additional 15-second intervals until smooth and spreadable. Dip edge of each cookie into candy; decorate as desired. Let stand on parchment paper 15 minutes or until set.

*Makes about 2 dozen cookies*

White Chocolate Shamrocks

# Easter Nest Cookies

1½ cups all-purpose flour
1 teaspoon baking powder
½ teaspoon salt
¾ cup (1½ sticks) butter
2 cups miniature marshmallows
½ cup sugar
1 egg white
1 teaspoon vanilla extract
½ teaspoon almond extract
3¾ cups MOUNDS® Sweetened Coconut Flakes, divided
JOLLY RANCHER® Jelly Beans
HERSHEY'S Candy-Coated Milk Chocolate Eggs

**1.** Heat oven to 375°F.

**2.** Stir together flour, baking powder and salt; set aside. Place butter and marshmallows in microwave-safe bowl. Microwave at HIGH (100%) 1 to 1½ minutes or just until mixture melts when stirred. Beat sugar, egg white, vanilla and almond extract in separate bowl; add melted butter mixture, beating until light and fluffy. Gradually add flour mixture, beating until blended. Stir in 2 cups coconut.

**3.** Shape dough into 1-inch balls; roll balls in remaining 1¾ cups coconut, tinting coconut, if desired.* Place balls on ungreased cookie sheet. Press thumb into center of each ball, creating shallow depression.

**4.** Bake 8 to 10 minutes or just until lightly browned. Place 1 to 3 jelly beans and milk chocolate eggs in center of each cookie. Transfer to wire rack; cool completely.

*Makes about 3½ dozen cookies*

*\*To tint coconut: Place ¾ teaspoon water and a few drops food color in small bowl; stir in 1¾ cups coconut. Toss with fork until evenly tinted; cover tightly.*

Easter Nest Cookies

# Earth Day Delights

3½ cups all-purpose flour
1 teaspoon salt
1½ cups sugar
1 cup (2 sticks) unsalted butter, softened
2 eggs
2 teaspoons vanilla
1½ cups chopped pecans
Royal Icing (recipe follows)
Blue and green gel food colorings

**1.** Whisk flour and salt in medium bowl. Beat sugar and butter in large bowl with electric mixer at medium speed until light and fluffy. Add eggs, 1 at a time, beating until blended after each addition. Add vanilla; beat until blended.

**2.** Gradually add flour mixture, beating until blended after each addition. Stir in pecans. Divide dough evenly into 2 discs. Wrap and refrigerate 1 hour.

**3.** Preheat oven to 350°F. Line cookie sheets with parchment paper. Working with 1 disc at a time, roll out dough between parchment paper to ⅜-inch thickness. Cut out circles with 3¼-inch round cookie cutter. Place 1 inch apart on prepared cookie sheets. Refrigerate 15 minutes.

**4.** Bake 15 to 17 minutes or until set. Cool on cookie sheets 5 minutes. Remove to wire racks; cool completely.

**5.** Prepare Royal Icing. Divide icing into 2 small bowls Add blue food coloring to 1 bowl, a few drops at a time; stir until evenly colored. Spread cookies with blue icing. Let stand 10 minutes or until set.

**6.** Add green food coloring, a few drops at a time, to remaining bowl; stir until evenly colored. Pipe continent shapes using green icing. Let stand 10 minutes or until set.

*Makes about 1½ dozen cookies*

Royal Icing: Combine 4 cups powdered sugar, 6 tablespoons water and 3 tablespoons meringue powder in medium bowl. Beat with electric mixer at high speed 7 to 10 minutes or until soft peaks form. Cover surface with plastic wrap until needed. Makes about 2 cups.

·Let's Celebrate·

Earth Day Delights

# Birthday Cake Cookies

1 package (about 16 ounces) refrigerated sugar cookie dough
Food coloring (optional)
1 container (16 ounces) prepared white frosting
Colored nonpareils or decors
10 small birthday candles

**1.** Preheat oven to 350°F. Lightly grease 10 mini (1¾-inch) muffin cups and 10 standard (2½-inch) muffin cups. Shape one third of dough into 10 (1-inch) balls; press into bottoms of prepared mini muffin cups. Shape remaining two thirds of dough into 10 equal balls; press into bottoms of prepared standard muffin cups.

**2.** Bake mini cookies 8 to 9 minutes or until edges are light brown. Bake standard cookies 10 to 11 minutes or until edges are light brown. Cool in pans 5 minutes. Remove to wire racks; cool completely.

**3.** Add food coloring, if desired, to frosting; mix well. Spread frosting over top and side of each cookie. Place 1 mini cookie on top of 1 standard cookie. Decorate with nonpareils. Press 1 candle into center of each cookie. *Makes 10 cookies*

*Tip* A great alternative to regular birthday cake, these single-serving treats will save you the time and mess it takes to cut all those slices during the party. Or, send them home with guests as party favors.

Birthday Cake Cookies

# Congrats Grad!

    1 package (about 16 ounces) refrigerated sugar cookie dough
    ¼ cup all-purpose flour
    ¼ cup creamy peanut butter
    1 cup mini semisweet chocolate chips
      Granulated sugar
    48 small gumdrops
      Cookie Glaze (recipe follows)
      Food coloring
    12 graham cracker squares

**1.** Let dough stand at room temperature 15 minutes. Lightly grease 12 standard (2½-inch) muffin cups.

**2.** Preheat oven to 350°F. Combine dough, flour and peanut butter in large bowl; beat with electric mixer at medium speed until well blended. Stir in chocolate chips. Shape dough into 12 balls; press into bottoms of prepared muffin cups.

**3.** Bake 15 to 18 minutes or until lightly browned. Cool in pan 10 minutes. Remove to wire rack; cool completely.

**4.** Sprinkle sugar on waxed paper. For each tassel, slightly flatten 3 gumdrops. Place gumdrops, with ends overlapping slightly, on sugared surface. Roll flattened gumdrops into 3×1-inch piece, turning over frequently to coat with sugar. Trim and discard edges of gumdrop piece. Cut piece into 2½×¼-inch strips. Cut bottom part into several lengthwise strips to form fringe.

**5.** Prepare Cookie Glaze. Tint glaze with food coloring as desired. Place cookies upside down on wire rack set over waxed paper. Spread glaze over cookies. Spread glaze over graham crackers; attach 1 cracker to top of each cookie. Place tassel on each cap. Set gumdrop on each tassel for cap button. Let stand 40 minutes or until set.     *Makes 1 dozen cookies*

**Cookie Glaze:** Combine 4 cups powdered sugar and 6 to 8 tablespoons milk, 1 tablespoon at a time, in medium bowl to make a pourable glaze. Makes about 2 cups.

Congrats Grad!

# Monogram Cookies

    3½ cups all-purpose flour
      1 teaspoon salt
    1½ cups sugar
      1 cup (2 sticks) unsalted butter, softened
      2 eggs
      2 teaspoons vanilla
        Gel food coloring
      1 container (16 ounces) white or vanilla frosting
        Assorted jumbo nonpareils

**1.** Whisk flour and salt in medium bowl.

**2.** Beat sugar and butter in large bowl with electric mixer at medium speed until light and fluffy. Add eggs, 1 at a time, beating until blended after each addition. Add vanilla; beat until blended.

**3.** Gradually add flour mixture, beating until blended after each addition. Divide dough evenly into 2 discs. Wrap and refrigerate 1 hour.

**4.** Preheat oven to 350°F. Line cookie sheets with parchment paper. Working with 1 disc at a time, roll out dough between parchment paper to ⅜-inch thickness. Cut out circles with 3-inch fluted round cookie cutter. Place 1 inch apart on prepared cookie sheets. Cut out letters using 1-inch alphabet cookie cutters; discard. Refrigerate 15 minutes.

**5.** Bake 15 to 17 minutes or until set. Cool on cookie sheets 5 minutes. Remove to wire racks; cool completely.

**6.** Add food coloring, a few drops at a time, to frosting; stir until evenly colored. Spread cookies with frosting. Decorate with nonpareils as desired. Let stand 10 minutes or until set.

*Makes 2 dozen cookies*

Monogram Cookies

# Liberty Bell Cookies

## Cookies

  2 packages (about 17 ounces each) sugar cookie mix
  ¼ cup all-purpose flour
  ⅔ cup unsalted butter, melted
  2 eggs

## Glaze

  ¼ cup powdered sugar
  1 teaspoon water
  ¼ teaspoon ground cinnamon
  ¼ teaspoon vanilla
    Brown decorating icing

**1.** Line cookie sheets with parchment paper. Combine cookie mix and flour in large bowl; stir well. Add butter and eggs; stir until well combined. Divide dough evenly into 2 discs. Wrap and refrigerate 1 hour.

**2.** Preheat oven to 375°F. Working with 1 disc at a time, roll out dough between parchment paper to ¼-inch thickness. Cut out shapes using 3-inch bell cookie cutter. Place 1 inch apart on prepared cookie sheets. Refrigerate 15 minutes.

**3.** Bake 10 to 12 minutes or until set. Cool on cookie sheets 5 minutes. Remove to wire racks; cool completely.

**4.** For glaze, combine powdered sugar, water, cinnamon and vanilla in small bowl; stir until smooth. Spread glaze on cookies. Let stand 15 minutes or until set. Outline bell and draw crack and clapper with decorating icing.           *Makes 3 dozen cookies*

**Variation:** You may use melted chocolate in place of the decorating icing. Place about 1 cup chocolate chips in resealable food storage bag (but do not seal). Microwave 30 seconds at a time until chocolate chips begin to soften and lose their shape. Remove from microwave, seal bag and knead until smooth. Snip off corner of bag and squeeze to outline bell and draw crack and clapper.

Liberty Bell Cookies

# Hanukkah Coin Cookies

1 cup (2 sticks) butter or margarine, softened
1 cup sugar
1 egg
1 teaspoon vanilla extract
1¾ cups all-purpose flour
½ cup HERSHEY'S Cocoa
1½ teaspoons baking powder
½ teaspoon salt
BUTTERCREAM FROSTING (recipe follows)

1. Beat butter, sugar, egg and vanilla in large bowl until well blended. Stir together flour, cocoa, baking powder and salt; gradually add to butter mixture, beating until well blended. Divide dough in half; place each half on separate sheet of wax paper.

2. Shape each portion into log, about 7 inches long. Wrap each log in wax paper or plastic wrap. Refrigerate until firm, at least 8 hours.

3. Heat oven to 325°F. Cut logs into ¼-inch-thick slices. Place on ungreased cookie sheet.

4. Bake 8 to 10 minutes or until set. Cool slightly; remove from cookie sheet to wire rack. Cool completely. Prepare BUTTERCREAM FROSTING; spread over tops of cookies.

*Makes about 4½ dozen cookies*

# Buttercream Frosting

¼ cup (½ stick) butter, softened
1½ cups powdered sugar
1 to 2 tablespoons milk
½ teaspoon vanilla extract
Yellow food color

Beat butter until creamy. Gradually add powdered sugar and milk to butter, beating to desired consistency. Stir in vanilla and food color.

*Makes about 1 cup frosting*

•Let's Celebrate•

Hanukkah Coin Cookies

# Buche De Noel Cookies

⅔ cup butter or margarine, softened
1 cup granulated sugar
2 eggs
2 teaspoons vanilla extract
2½ cups all-purpose flour
½ cup HERSHEY'S Cocoa
½ teaspoon baking soda
¼ teaspoon salt
MOCHA FROSTING (recipe follows)
Powdered sugar (optional)

**1.** Beat butter and granulated sugar with electric mixer on medium speed in large bowl until well blended. Add eggs and vanilla; beat until fluffy. Stir together flour, cocoa, baking soda and salt; gradually add to butter mixture, beating until well blended. Cover; refrigerate dough 1 to 2 hours.

**2.** Heat oven to 350°F. Shape heaping teaspoons of dough into logs about 2½ inches long and ¾ inch in diameter; place on ungreased cookie sheet. Bake 7 to 9 minutes or until set. Cool slightly. Remove to wire rack and cool completely.

**3.** Frost cookies with MOCHA FROSTING. Using tines of fork, draw lines through frosting to imitate tree bark. Lightly dust with powdered sugar, if desired.

*Makes about 2½ dozen cookies*

# Mocha Frosting

6 tablespoons butter or margarine, softened
2⅔ cups powdered sugar
⅓ cup HERSHEY'S Cocoa
3 to 4 tablespoons milk
2 teaspoons powdered instant espresso dissolved in 1 teaspoon hot water
1 teaspoon vanilla extract

*continued on page 104*

·Let's Celebrate·

Buche De Noel Cookies

*Buche De Noel Cookies, continued*

Beat butter with electric mixer on medium speed in medium bowl until creamy. Add powdered sugar and cocoa alternately with milk, dissolved espresso and vanilla, beating to spreadable consistency. *Makes about 1²/₃ cups frosting*

# Sparkling Sugar Cookie Snowmen

   1 container (16 ounces) prepared vanilla frosting
   1 bag (8.6 ounces) PEPPERIDGE FARM® Soft Baked Sugar Cookies
   1 jar (2.25 ounces) blue crystal decorative sugar
½ cup granulated sugar
   1 bag (12 ounces) candy-coated mini baking pieces
   8 miniature marshmallows, cut in half

**1.** Spread some of the frosting over the entire top of each cookie, at least ¹/₁₆ inch thick.

**2.** Holding each cookie over a paper plate, generously sprinkle blue sugar on the upper third of the frosting. Shake off extra sugar away from the plain frosting onto the plate. Gently pat the sugar into the frosting.

**3.** Holding each cookie over a different paper plate, generously sprinkle granulated sugar on remaining frosting. Shake off extra sugar away from the blue area onto the plate. Gently pat the sugar into frosting.

**4.** Attach a small plain decorating tip (#4) to a pastry bag* and fill halfway with frosting. Pipe the frosting in circular or up and down motion across the edge of blue to form the "fur" trim of the snowman's hat. Press in 2 candy-coated pieces just under the "fur" for the eyes. Press in 1 candy-coated piece in the center for the nose. Press 4 candy-coated pieces to form a smile. Place a marshmallow half cut-side down into the frosting at the top of the blue section for the hat's pom-pom. *Makes 8 cookies*

*Or use a resealable small plastic bag. Cut off one corner to make a small opening.

Sparkling Sugar Cookie Snowmen

# Cookie Creations

## Marshmallow Chipper Cookie Cake

3½ cups all-purpose flour
1 teaspoon baking powder
1 teaspoon baking soda
1 teaspoon salt
1 cup packed light brown sugar
½ cup granulated sugar
3 cups (6 sticks) unsalted butter, softened, divided
2 eggs
2 egg yolks
2 teaspoons vanilla, divided
2 cups (12 ounces) semisweet chocolate chips
2 cups powdered sugar
2 containers (7 ounces each) marshmallow creme

1. Whisk flour, baking powder, baking soda and salt in medium bowl. Combine brown sugar and granulated sugar in large bowl. Add 1 cup (2 sticks) butter; beat with electric mixer at medium speed until light and fluffy. Add eggs, 1 at a time, beating until blended after each addition. Add egg yolks and 1 teaspoon vanilla; beat until blended.

2. Gradually add flour mixture, beating until blended after each addition. Stir in chocolate chips. Divide dough evenly into 3 discs. Wrap and refrigerate overnight.

3. Preheat oven to 325°F. Line cookie sheets with parchment paper. Working with 1 disc at a time, roll out dough between parchment paper into 8-inch circle about ½ inch thick. Transfer to prepared cookie sheets; refrigerate 15 minutes.

*continued on page 108*

**4.** Bake 25 to 27 minutes or until light brown and set. Cool on cookie sheets 5 minutes. Remove to wire racks; cool completely.

**5.** Beat remaining 2 cups (4 sticks) butter in another large bowl at medium speed until smooth. Gradually add powdered sugar, beating until blended after each addition. Beat at high speed 2 minutes or until light and fluffy. Add remaining 1 teaspoon vanilla; beat until blended. Stir in marshmallow creme.

**6.** Place 1 cookie on serving plate. Spread with half of marshmallow mixture. Repeat layers. Top with remaining cookie. Cover; refrigerate 1 hour before slicing.

*Makes 16 to 20 servings*

# Lollipop Flower Pots

1 package (about 16 ounces) refrigerated sugar cookie dough
36 caramels
1 cup chocolate cookie crumbs
Green gummy fruit slices or candy spearmint leaves
36 small lollipops

**1.** Preheat oven to 350°F. Lightly grease 36 mini (1¾-inch) muffin cups. Shape dough into 36 balls; press onto bottoms and up sides of prepared muffin cups. Place 1 caramel in center of each muffin cup.

**2.** Bake 10 to 11 minutes or until edges are lightly browned. Cool in pans 2 minutes. Remove to wire racks; cool completely.

**3.** Sprinkle cookie crumbs evenly into center of cookies. Flatten gummy fruit slices slightly; press into leaf shapes. Push 1 lollipop and 2 leaves into each cookie.

*Makes 3 dozen cookies*

Lollipop Flower Pots

# Surprise Cookies

2 squares (1 ounce each) semisweet baking chocolate, coarsely chopped
1¼ cups all-purpose flour
½ teaspoon baking powder
¼ teaspoon salt
½ cup (1 stick) butter, softened
½ cup sugar
1 egg
1 teaspoon vanilla
   Fillings: well-drained maraschino cherries or candied cherries; chocolate mint candies, broken into halves; white chocolate baking bar, cut into chunks; milk chocolate candy bar, cut into chunks; semisweet chocolate chunks; raspberry jam; or apricot preserves
   Sprinkles or nonpareils (optional)

**1.** Preheat oven to 350°F. Lightly grease 12 mini (1¾-inch) muffin cups.

**2.** Melt chocolate in small heavy saucepan over low heat, stirring constantly; remove from heat. Combine flour, baking powder and salt in small bowl.

**3.** Beat butter and sugar in large bowl with electric mixer at medium speed 2 minutes or until light and fluffy. Beat in egg and vanilla. Beat in melted chocolate. Gradually add flour mixture, beating at low speed until blended after each addition.

**4.** Drop dough by level teaspoonfuls into prepared muffin cups. Form small indentation in center of batter. Fill as desired with assorted fillings. Top with heaping teaspoonful of dough, smoothing top lightly. Top with sprinkles, if desired.

**5.** Bake 15 to 17 minutes or until set. Cool completely in pan.          *Makes 1 dozen cookies*

Tip: Store these cookies tightly covered at room temperature. They do not freeze well.

Surprise Cookies

# Chocolate Swirl Lollipop Cookies

½ cup (1 stick) butter or margarine, softened
1 cup sugar
2 eggs
1 teaspoon orange extract
1 teaspoon vanilla extract
2¼ cups all-purpose flour, divided
½ teaspoon baking soda
½ teaspoon salt
¼ teaspoon freshly grated orange peel
Few drops red and yellow food color (optional)
2 sections (½ ounce each) HERSHEY'S Unsweetened Chocolate Baking Bar, melted
About 24 wooden popsicle sticks

**1.** Beat butter and sugar in large bowl until blended. Add eggs and extracts; beat until light and fluffy. Gradually add 1¼ cups flour, blending until smooth. Stir in remaining 1 cup flour, baking soda and salt until mixture is well blended.

**2.** Place half of batter in medium bowl; stir in orange peel. Stir in food color, if desired. Melt chocolate as directed on package; stir into remaining half of batter. Cover; refrigerate both mixtures until firm enough to roll.

**3.** With rolling pin or fingers, between 2 pieces of wax paper, roll chocolate and orange mixtures each into 10×8-inch rectangle. Remove wax paper; place orange mixture on top of chocolate. Starting on longest side, roll up doughs tightly, forming into 12-inch roll; wrap in plastic wrap. Refrigerate until firm.

**4.** Heat oven to 350°F. Remove plastic wrap from roll; cut into ½-inch-wide slices. Place on cookie sheet at least 3 inches apart. Insert popsicle stick into each cookie.

**5.** Bake 8 to 10 minutes or until cookie is almost set. Cool slightly; remove from cookie sheet to wire rack. Cool completely. Decorate and tie with ribbon, if desired.

*Makes about 24 cookies*

·Cookie Creations·

Chocolate Swirl Lollipop Cookies

# Freaky Fruity Fish Bowl Cookie

  1 package (about 16 ounces) refrigerated sugar cookie dough
  2 packages (8 ounces each) cream cheese, softened
  ⅓ cup milk
  ⅔ cup powdered sugar
  ½ teaspoon vanilla
    Blue food coloring
    Blueberries
    Canned mandarin oranges, well drained and patted dry
    Green seedless grapes, sliced lengthwise and patted dry
    Gummy fish candies
    Sea creature fruit snacks
    Assorted colored decorating sugars

**1.** Preheat oven to 350°F. Coat cookie sheet with nonstick cooking spray.

**2.** Reserve one fourth of dough; set aside. Place remaining dough on prepared cookie sheet; flatten into 11×9-inch oval. Shape reserved dough into 2×12-inch strip and place on top of oval to make fish bowl shape.

**3.** Bake 13 minutes or until set. Cool completely on cookie sheet.

**4.** For frosting, beat cream cheese and milk in medium bowl with electric mixer at medium speed until blended. Add powdered sugar and vanilla; beat at low speed until smooth. Reserve ⅓ cup frosting in small bowl. Add food coloring, a few drops at a time, to remaining frosting; beat until evenly colored.

**5.** Spread blue frosting over "bowl" area and reserved white frosting over "rim" area of cookie.

**6.** Decorate cookie with fruit, gummy candies, fruit snacks and decorating sugars as desired.

*Makes 16 servings*

·Cookie Creations·

Freaky Fruity Fish Bowl Cookie

# Tea Party Cookies

1 package (about 16 ounces) refrigerated sugar cookie dough
¼ cup all-purpose flour
1 teaspoon apple pie spice*
   Almond Royal Icing (recipe follows)
   Assorted food colorings, candy fruit slices and assorted decors and sprinkles

*Substitute ½ teaspoon ground cinnamon, ¼ teaspoon ground nutmeg and ⅛ teaspoon ground allspice or ground cloves for 1 teaspoon apple pie spice.

**1.** Let dough stand at room temperature 15 minutes. Grease 6 jumbo (3-inch) muffin cups.

**2.** Preheat oven to 350°F. Combine dough, flour and apple pie spice in large bowl; beat with electric mixer at medium speed until well blended. Reserve half of dough; wrap and refrigerate.

**3.** For cups, shape remaining dough into 6 balls; press onto bottoms and up sides of muffin cups. Freeze 10 minutes. Bake 8 minutes. Immediately press cookies against sides and bottoms of muffin cups to reshape using back of lightly floured spoon. Bake 5 to 7 minutes; press with back of lightly floured spoon to reshape. Cool in pan 3 minutes. Remove to wire rack; cool completely.

**4.** For saucers, shape reserved dough into 6 (3-inch) discs. Place 2 inches apart on ungreased cookie sheet. Bake 7 minutes or until edges are lightly browned. Press down center of saucers with back of lightly floured spoon. Cool on cookie sheet 3 minutes. Remove to wire rack; cool completely.

**5.** Prepare Almond Royal Icing; spread evenly on inside of cups. Let stand 30 minutes or until set. Tint remaining icing desired colors; spread on outside of cups and saucers. Attach 1 fruit slice to each cup with icing for handle. Decorate with decors and sprinkles as desired. Let stand 30 minutes or until set. To serve, place 1 cup cookie on each saucer cookie.

*Makes 6 cup cookies and 6 saucer cookies*

Almond Royal Icing: Beat 2 egg whites in medium bowl with electric mixer at high speed until foamy. Gradually add 4 cups powdered sugar and almond extract. Beat at low speed until moistened. Beat at high speed until stiff, adding additional powdered sugar if necessary. Makes about 2 cups.

Tea Party Cookies

# Whirligigs

   1 package (about 16 ounces) refrigerated sugar cookie dough
   ¼ cup all-purpose flour
   ½ teaspoon *each* banana and strawberry extract (optional)
      Yellow and red food colorings
      Colored sugar (optional)
   12 (8-inch) lollipop sticks or wooden popsicle sticks*

*\*Lollipop sticks and popsicle sticks are available at craft stores and where cake decorating supplies are sold.*

**1.** Let dough stand at room temperature 15 minutes. Grease cookie sheets.

**2.** Combine dough and flour in large bowl; beat with electric mixer at medium speed until well blended. Divide dough in half; place in separate medium bowls. Add banana extract, if desired, and yellow food coloring to dough in 1 bowl. Add strawberry extract, if desired, and red food coloring to dough in remaining bowl. Beat doughs separately at medium speed until well blended. Shape each dough into disc; wrap and freeze 30 minutes.

**3.** Preheat oven to 350°F. Shape red dough into rope about 18 inches long on lightly floured surface. Repeat with yellow dough. Twist ropes together. Divide rope into 3 equal pieces. Working with 1 piece at a time, shape dough into rope about 20 inches long. Cut into 4 equal pieces. Coil each piece into circle; place 2 inches apart on prepared cookie sheets. (Make sure to leave room for lollipop sticks.) Sprinkle cookies with colored sugar, if desired. Refrigerate 15 minutes.

**4.** Carefully press lollipop stick into edge of each cookie. Bake 12 to 15 minutes or until set. Cool completely on cookie sheets.                    *Makes 1 dozen cookies*

Whirligigs

# Sweetheart Chocolate Pizza

5 squares BAKER'S® Semi-Sweet Baking Chocolate, divided
1 package (16.5 ounces) refrigerated sugar cookie dough
1 cup cold milk
1 package (4-serving size) JELL-O® Chocolate Flavor Instant Pudding & Pie Filling
¼ cup powdered sugar
1 tub (8 ounces) COOL WHIP® Whipped Topping, thawed, divided
1½ cups halved strawberries

PREHEAT oven to 375°F. Place 4 of the chocolate squares in medium microwaveable bowl. Microwave on high 2 minutes, stirring after 1 minute. Stir until completely melted. Add cookie dough; mix until well blended. Press onto bottom of ungreased 12-inch pizza pan. Bake 10 minutes. Cool completely.

POUR milk into medium bowl. Add dry pudding mix and sugar. Beat with wire whisk 2 minutes or until well blended. Gently stir in half of the whipped topping. Spread evenly over crust.

SPREAD remaining whipped topping in heart shape over pudding layer. Decorate with strawberries. Melt remaining chocolate square as directed on package; drizzle evenly over dessert. Let stand until chocolate is firm. Cut dessert into wedges to serve. Store leftover dessert in refrigerator. *Makes 12 servings, 1 wedge each.*

Make It Easy: To make decorating the dessert easier, spoon whipped topping into resealable plastic bag; seal bag. Snip off small piece from one of the bottom corners of bag; pipe into heart shape on top of dessert.

Prep Time: 20 minutes
Total Time: 1 hour (includes cooling)

·Cookie Creations·

Sweetheart Chocolate Pizza

# Snapshot Cookies

3½ cups all-purpose flour
1 teaspoon salt
1½ cups sugar
1 cup (2 sticks) unsalted butter, softened
2 eggs
2 teaspoons vanilla
Royal Icing (recipe follows)
Black gel food coloring, assorted colored round candies and mini gummy candies

**1.** Whisk flour and salt in medium bowl. Beat sugar and butter in large bowl with electric mixer at medium speed until light and fluffy. Add eggs, 1 at a time, beating until blended after each addition. Add vanilla; beat until blended. Gradually add flour mixture, beating until blended after each addition. Divide dough evenly into 2 discs. Wrap and refrigerate 1 hour.

**2.** Preheat oven to 350°F. Line cookie sheets with parchment paper. Working with 1 disc at a time, roll out dough between parchment paper to ⅜-inch thickness. From each disc, cut out 6 rectangles with sharp knife (approximately 2½×3½-inch shapes) and 6 circles with 1½-inch round cookie cutter.

**3.** Place rectangles 2 inches apart on prepared cookie sheets. Place circles 1 inch apart on separate prepared cookie sheet. Refrigerate 15 minutes. Bake rectangles 15 to 17 minutes or until set. Bake circles 12 to 15 minutes or until set. Cool on cookie sheets 5 minutes. Remove to wire racks; cool completely.

**4.** Prepare Royal Icing. Reserve 1 cup Royal Icing. Add food coloring, a few drops at a time, to remaining icing; stir until evenly colored. Spread rectangles with black icing. Let stand 10 minutes or until set. Spread circles with reserved white icing. Spread thin layer of white icing on back of circles and adhere to rectangles for lens. Let stand 10 minutes or until set.

**5.** Dot back of round candies with icing and adhere for flash, viewfinder and lens. Dot back of gummy candy with icing and adhere to side of rectangle for button. Let stand 10 minutes or until set.

*Makes 1 dozen cookies*

**Royal Icing:** Combine 4 cups powdered sugar, 6 tablespoons water and 3 tablespoons meringue powder in medium bowl. Beat with electric mixer at high speed 7 to 10 minutes or until soft peaks form. Cover surface with plastic wrap until needed. Makes about 2 cups.

## •Cookie Creations•

Snapshot Cookies

# Christmas Cookie Tree

2 packages (about 16 ounces each) refrigerated sugar cookie dough
2 to 3 tubes (about 4 ounces each) green decorating icing with tips
1 tube (about 4 ounces) yellow decorating icing
1 tube (about 4 ounces) red decorating icing

**1.** Preheat oven to 350°F. Line 2 cookie sheets with parchment paper.

**2.** Let 1 package dough stand at room temperature 15 minutes. Roll out dough between parchment paper to ¼-inch thickness. Cut out 7-inch circle* and 6½-inch circle using sharp knife. Transfer circles to prepared cookie sheet. Reserve scraps; wrap and refrigerate.

**3.** Repeat step 2 with remaining package dough, cutting out 6-inch circle and 5½-inch circle. Transfer to separate prepared cookie sheet. Bake 10 to 14 minutes or until edges are lightly browned. Cool on cookies sheets 2 minutes. Remove parchment paper to wire racks; cool completely before removing from parchment paper.

**4.** Repeat step 3, using scraps to make 8 more circles, each ½ inch smaller in diameter. Reduce baking time as circles get smaller.

**5.** To assemble tree, secure largest cookie to serving platter with frosting. Using leaf tip and green icing, pipe leaves around outer edge of cookie. Place small amount of icing in center of cookie. Add next biggest cookie and repeat layers, adding cookies largest to smallest.

**6.** Pipe garlands around tree using yellow icing. Pipe ornaments using red icing.

**7.** Serve cookies individually by separating layers or cut into pieces using serrated knife.

*Makes 12 to 15 servings*

*\*Use a compass to draw 12 circles, each one ½ inch smaller, on parchment paper; cut out and use as patterns to cut dough circles. For a free-form look, use various bowls, glasses and biscuit cutters to trace and cut out 12 graduated circles.*

Christmas Cookie Tree

# Acknowledgments

Campbell Soup Company

The Hershey Company

Kraft Foods Inc.

© Mars, Incorporated 2010

The Quaker® Oatmeal Kitchens

·Index·

# METRIC CONVERSION CHART

## VOLUME MEASUREMENTS (dry)

1/8 teaspoon = 0.5 mL
1/4 teaspoon = 1 mL
1/2 teaspoon = 2 mL
3/4 teaspoon = 4 mL
1 teaspoon = 5 mL
1 tablespoon = 15 mL
2 tablespoons = 30 mL
1/4 cup = 60 mL
1/3 cup = 75 mL
1/2 cup = 125 mL
2/3 cup = 150 mL
3/4 cup = 175 mL
1 cup = 250 mL
2 cups = 1 pint = 500 mL
3 cups = 750 mL
4 cups = 1 quart = 1 L

## VOLUME MEASUREMENTS (fluid)

1 fluid ounce (2 tablespoons) = 30 mL
4 fluid ounces (1/2 cup) = 125 mL
8 fluid ounces (1 cup) = 250 mL
12 fluid ounces (1 1/2 cups) = 375 mL
16 fluid ounces (2 cups) = 500 mL

## WEIGHTS (mass)

1/2 ounce = 15 g
1 ounce = 30 g
3 ounces = 90 g
4 ounces = 120 g
8 ounces = 225 g
10 ounces = 285 g
12 ounces = 360 g
16 ounces = 1 pound = 450 g

## DIMENSIONS

1/16 inch = 2 mm
1/8 inch = 3 mm
1/4 inch = 6 mm
1/2 inch = 1.5 cm
3/4 inch = 2 cm
1 inch = 2.5 cm

## OVEN TEMPERATURES

250°F = 120°C
275°F = 140°C
300°F = 150°C
325°F = 160°C
350°F = 180°C
375°F = 190°C
400°F = 200°C
425°F = 220°C
450°F = 230°C

## BAKING PAN SIZES

| Utensil | Size in Inches/Quarts | Metric Volume | Size in Centimeters |
|---|---|---|---|
| Baking or | 8×8×2 | 2 L | 20×20×5 |
| Cake Pan | 9×9×2 | 2.5 L | 23×23×5 |
| (square or | 12×8×2 | 3 L | 30×20×5 |
| rectangular) | 13×9×2 | 3.5 L | 33×23×5 |
| Loaf Pan | 8×4×3 | 1.5 L | 20×10×7 |
| | 9×5×3 | 2 L | 23×13×7 |
| Round Layer | 8×1½ | 1.2 L | 20×4 |
| Cake Pan | 9×1½ | 1.5 L | 23×4 |
| Pie Plate | 8×1¼ | 750 mL | 20×3 |
| | 9×1¼ | 1 L | 23×3 |
| Baking Dish | 1 quart | 1 L | — |
| or Casserole | 1½ quart | 1.5 L | — |
| | 2 quart | 2 L | — |